INUA ELLAMS

Born in Nigeria, Inua Ellams is a UK-based poet, playwright and performer who has written for the Royal Shakespeare Company, the National Theatre and the BBC. His latest play was an adaptation of Chekhov's *Three Sisters* set in Nigeria, staged at the National Theatre. *The Actual* is Ellams' fifth poetry release, and first full collection, after *Thirteen Fairy Negro Tales* (flipped eye, 2005), *Candy Coated Unicorns and Converse All Stars* (flipped eye, 2011), *The Wire-Headed Heathen* (Akashic Books, 2016) and *The Half God of Rainfall* (Fourth Estate, 2019).

ALSO BY INUA ELLAMS

POETRY

#Afterhours (Nine Arches Press, 2017)
The Wire-Headed Heathen (Akashic Books, 2016)
Candy Coated Unicorns and Converse All Stars (flipped eye, 2011)
Thirteen Fairy Negro Tales (flipped eye, 2005)

DRAMA

Three Sisters (Oberon, 2019)
The Half God of Rainfall (Fourth Estate, 2019)
Barber Shop Chronicles (Oberon, 2017)
The 14th Tale (Oberon, 2015)
Cape (Oberon, 2013)
Black T-Shirt Collection (Oberon, 2012)
Knight Watch (Oberon, 2012)
Untitled (Oberon, 2010)

The Actual

Inua Ellams

Penned in the Margins

LONDON

PUBLISHED BY PENNED IN THE MARGINS
Toynbee Studios, 28 Commercial Street, London E1 6AB
www.pennedinthemargins.co.uk

The right of Inua Ellams to be identified as the author of this work has been asserted by him in accordance with Section 77 of the Copyright, Designs and Patent Act 1988.

First published 2020

Printed in the United Kingdom by TJ International

ISBN
978-1-908058-78-2

CONTENTS

This is *still, still, still,* dedicated
to the capsules of walking water
/ sculpted by the wind

The Actual / ~~Fuck~~

POEMS

Fuck / *Tupac*

for dying early / for the fields of lavender and hawthorn in which
I sat / overlooking Dublin City / though / as dusk wrapped the
sky / it could have been any creaking constellation of traffic and
tower blocks / from Compton to Clondalkin / blinking staccato
madness / into the unspooling night / Fuck you / for forcing
the criminal animal gnashing its teeth in piss-streaked alleys /
collarless priests cruising in rented hatchbacks / Protestants and
Catholics / like Bloods and Crips / brothers split along colour
lines / fuelled by racist police / who came to break our skin /
Fuck you / for ordering them / to the rank and file of rhyme /
for making sense of the Celtic anarchy / in those urban psalms
of your slim scripture / in your rich voice / explaining / this is
how it's always been / darkness / light / thin paths between / with
you leading / you reluctant messiah / as all true messiahs must
be / leading to a fellowship of souls / hunkered in headphones /
suspended between word and hard matter / fans / disciples / self-
sanctified street-saints / thrown stones of strange fruit / sour as we
are / scattered across the tar-marked planet / haloed in snapbacks
/ hooded / hidden / hollering hard / hallelujah-ring / head bowed
/ nodding in pious agreement / How we would have followed you
/ homie / to hell and back / How you had me / whole

Fuck / *Biggie Too*

I've never had a nemesis / question my manhood / never had
its length drawn out / between teeth / like beef / spat out / in
backyards and bedrooms / streets and stoops / from Ballycragh to
Brooklyn and back / Never had kids / scowl / at the mere sound of
my name / But because I've looked in the mirror and felt / unlike
the man who looked back / half empty / as though my spirit
found my flesh vacuous and slack / loose as a twig in a drum's
hollow / I know what it is to search outside oneself / for grit and
grandeur to fill in the emptiness / I know what it is / however ill
advised / to swallow what pith and poisoned pasture the world
fields for Black men / to swell into a trembling mountain of skin
and pressed silence / to guard the treacherous fragility of such
girth / and swagger with it / through those same backyards and
bedrooms / streets and stoops / eyes peeled for the night's glinting
teeth / anxious / twitching / as if a wild thing / born again yet
ready to die

Fuck / *The Mandela Effect*

#After Danez Smith

Noun / Definition / Confabulation / collective misremembering of events or details / named after an imprisoned African activist / thought deceased in the mid '80s / who when released later / lead his nation / Tell me how it is possible to forget a country sized man / how one misremembers mountains breathing / Black men are killed so often / it's assumed we've already passed / Whole White worlds imagine us in coffins / our skin the colour of stained wood / No wonder police have skittish fingers / How else would you react to a corpse / walking / Wouldn't you think yourself seeing things / perhaps the wicked metal of a gun / a knife's simmering silver smile / even in our empty open palms / our fingers splayed like an asterisk / to draw attention to our humanity / our Black lives still mattering / Let them call us Nigger / we can reclaim such cruel breath in verse / Let them raze our villages to dust / we will sculpt the mud to houses / Let them burn our sugarcane fields / we are already part molasses / To be Black is to constantly achieve the improbable / to drive unchallenged through your own neighbourhood / to return home safe with sweets / to keep your name intact / to be safe jogging / to breathe / to breathe / to breathe / but some miracles are better left performed once / Dear

God of language and narrative / having sent back your patched-up son / black / holy and bruised / restrict some of that which you have given / Some folks are too loose with words / Don't let them call us dead

Fuck / *Mandela*

Found poem /

So / Winnie Mandela should have led this country / It's because of her he was freed / She said let's render South Africa ungovernable / fuck it up / so Whites have no choice but to back down / That's why they freed Mandela and he let them off easy / Truth and Reconciliation Commission was a farce / A year of countless Blacks coming forward saying my father was murdered / brother tortured / son mutilated / all the perpetrators had to do was admit it or apologise / most didn't even do that / They said they were taking orders / in a war situation / For us it was genocide / Look at our society / The fact we never got to deal with it manifests in violence / men who rape children / beat women / If criminals hijack a car / they slit the driver's throat / We are still frustrated / Generations emasculated / called Boys for centuries / taking it out on each other because we never got to get mad and say we were fucked around / for 350 years and no one was held accountable / I don't want sympathy / It's time for them to pay / A recent survey showed 40% of White South Africans don't think / apartheid was wrong / This is the world we live in / The balance of economic power is with them / in our own land / Mandela failed us / Am I wrong

Fuck / *Sympathy*

Because Christ was the first Black man lynched / who went viral / and what the world did was white / wash / his / story such that his fingers splayed / his hands raised / his body bolted with wicked metal / to a cross / is hoisted over the very folk it is said he died for / to preach to us some turn the other cheek shit / Because we are still dying as he did / I've begun to reject thoughts and sympathetic fucking prayers willed to the family of the deceased / Fuck each headline's weak hug / the spokesperson's measured words / Fuck waiting for police / whole systems of governance / down to a filing cabinet's labelling minutiae / to deinstitutionalise its relentless racism / Naaa fam / I'm on some other shit / I've begun to construct an absurdist fantasy / naaa fam / a safe haven / dark as a cave's soul / the ocean is a sloe-brewed tincture / skies the colour of cloaked coal / soil as if soot / the constellations are a conglomerate of dark crystals / the moon's sliver is the light through Christ's wounds / Everything is black / All black everything / ripplegrass in fields / every tree's trunk / the sap swirling within / the branch / the lovely leaves / the flesh of fruit / the split seed / To bite is to make of your mouth a closed cove of a shrine / an altar in which your tongue laps at black water / shakes with our dead / ever much you drink / the thirst is never quenched

Fuck / *Weak Hugs*

The brain is a muscled residue of the cosmos / of dark matter and minuscule cells / so spun from galaxies / what swirls inside also evades our sharpest probes / Our best minds / can't fathom their dimmest lights / zipping in their fleshy millions / each thought a meteor rain / a cascading down of innumerable flares / This one compels my arms to hold your conglomerate of galaxies to mine / It means my world of worlds recognises yours / wills you life and primordial warmth / But when your arms are slow to rise / limp to embrace / the part of me that dies / the surprise / that startled wisp of air on my lips / is a gossamer necklace of planets passing / a whole solar system gone

Fuck / *Limp Handshakes*

You should do like this / Your four fingers should lift and hold whose hand you grip / You're saying I got you / you're got / as your thumb completes the lock / You push down as if leaving your thumb print / as if gifting its tiny terrain of hills and valleys / your self's singular geography / your soul's surface code / for this occasion of meeting / You wait until you feel a response / then lift your eyes to find its accompanying gaze / You hold / You squeeze tighter / Again you give of your land / give of your fibre / You're saying / remember me / as I will you

All through childhood / you practise before a mirror / diligently imagining / a truce in civil war / a father reconciling an estranged son / two media moguls merging their worlds / You bring such weight to first handshakes / only to reach out now and what grasps you back / is weak as cooked noodle / limp as warm slug / frail a stale celery / what the actual fuck

Fuck / *Borders*

The travellers of woods and waters who left by foot and paddle / who formed horse and saddle / rudder and sail / forged steam and engine and reached the holy grail of flight / So instinctive was collective strive / to boldly go / and yet go further / they went off-world / zoomed off-planet

The forestspiritchild in them who saw no borders in the sky / the winged wondering wild within / is who we have ever been / In time we'll wake to see the lines / these thin boundaries we have drawn / as utter folly and call out why / and when / and who / and how

Fuck / *Border Guards*

Heavy-booted and uniformed / the armed who man the borders / of narrative and myth / who cast the war-torn and hungry / as vermin / will say / he reached too far / dared dream broader than his country / than wings could carry / That chant of his / that song of light / was foreign / Sounded like a battle cry / too much like jihad / Icarus' whole flight / was ill advised / The father should have known better / Nothing can be done / Nothing / as he plunged

Fuck / *Shakespeare*

And another thing / the grace you brought Othello / how you forged that Moor / got him talking down his eloquence as if his tongue wasn't part swan feather / part molasses / how you wrote a church of darkness steepled by Iago / and Ol' Thello its soul beacon of honour and light / Bruh / that shit literary fire / race-theory brimstone / middle-passage gold

but /

how you played Caliban / his tongue as Othello's / and just as wronged / How you imbibed him with / emblemed him of colonised peoples / got me all riled up / imagining my ancestor's vengeance / a rough blade thrust through Prospero's proud heart / but you didn't / Play ends / Cali still enslaved / Bruh / that shit fucked

Fuck / *Perseus*

Regarding the claim / some women enable sexual predators / consider power structures / consider Mount Olympus / a gleaming symbol / of aspiration / of masculinity / so toxic / when Poseidon raped the mortal maiden Medusa / in Athena's smaller temple / Athena cursed its defilement / blamed Medusa / turned her scaly-skinned / snaked-headed / of such ugliness / to see her was to freeze the blood / to stone

then Perseus comes along / all swashbuckling bastard / all gleaming-shielded schmuck / to slay her / slice her / spear her swirling skull / and all the men cheered / and Poseidon stayed silent / his crime forgotten when Perseus won / And story by story / myth by myth / urban legend by urban legend / locker room talk by locker room talk / men make other men

Fuck / *Tommy Robinson*

Because theirs is a progressive work / Tommy / you are less than / less even than their slimy spirits / indeed / you are what the slimy spirits of maggots are spooked with / Before birth / maggotspiritmothers tuck into rotting food and decomposing flesh / spirits of their young / warning / If you consider bad deeds / You'll be born without the enzymes we ooze to melt food / Or worse / the mothers warn / You'll become Tommy Robinson / In life / all the while chomping through decaying flesh / feasting on their wounded brethren / they chant / I'm not Tommy Robinson / I'm not Tommy Robinson / like field slave work songs / pushing them through their celestial necessary murky work / to pupal stage / to eventual resurrection / where their spirits evolve upwards / unfurling into flies / their thorax emerald chrome / eyes burnished burgundy / their wings see-through blue and glazed with lightning

Fuck / *#45*

Though you've held his nicknames like bullets in your throat / Adolf Twitler / though you've loaded each chamber / Grabba The Hut / cocked back your tongue / Dubious Caesar / and let each shell blast the frustrated silence / Hairman Mao / though you are ever gun-ready / good to shoot from the lip and the crew you roll with always come correct / Hair Hitler / Ghenghis Can't / Vanilla ISIS / Toupee Fiasco / Clickwork Orange / though you chorus these / forthright as baptist hymns / making fellowship and communion of collective laughter / it's the night crossing the odd part of a town / in another country a world away / on a street ravenous as morgues / barefooted dead-eyed White boys calls you / Nigger / as if a fact / as if their birthright / you learn the futility of laughter / its porous shield / that words can slip through / can still break you / its power affirmed / let loose in the wild / and this too Trump has done

Fuck / *#76*

#After Wayne Holloway Smith

There is the poet Theresa L. who is half quantum furnace half amazing / The social worker Theresa I. whose laughter is a coven of skinny-dipping witches / The field hand Theresa S. who shakes the dawn from its covers / The teacher Theresa D. whose heart is a fallen country / The compassionate Theresa C. the police could no longer afford / The nurse Theresa E. who prised my sister from cancer's jaws / The community kitchen cook Theresa R. who brews magic outta beans and roots / and so many others who curse their muddied name / Look how they stand / grim-faced / silent / jury of a unanimous guilty verdict / a cathedral of Theresas / a stadium full / lead by the Mother Theresa herself / her middle digit like a little stick of dynamite / their eyes locked on / Theresa May

Fuck / *#77*

When we mention you called all women naturally fickle / our men cannibals / our cousins pickaninnies / our smiles watermelon / our aunties letter boxes / our fathers tank-topped bum boys / our working-class uncles feckless / our single mothers uppity / their children ill-raised and ignorant / you claim to have done so in contexts / but refuse to acknowledge the goons who come along / their knuckles dragging / to hurl your words at people of colour passing / at immigrants / the working class / the vulnerable / who duck / under fire / as your contexts shatter above their heads / shards showering their flesh / Look how they hold each other as an act of rebellion / close ranks around their young / whose foreheads glitter / dappled with blood / trying to laugh into the day's gaping mouth / to present a brave front / preserve their dignity / traditions / culture / No harsh words / they whisper / to their petrified young / Respect your elders / they urge / But not him / they concede / Not you

Fuck / *Nestlé*

Mariam laughing that she'd started lactating / become fountain of youth / her body a freestanding factory for one / calls months later / when in the closed cave of her son's mouth / a tooth poked through / glimmering white and wet as starlight / wise men followed to Bethlehem / and what's a mouth if not moist galaxy / what's milk if not primordial waters / what's a mother's chest if not Eden / and what is breastfeeding if not the passing of divine knowledge / the baby latching on / learning the body's soft frontier of flesh / The tongue's first and foremost purpose is this language / and then often times their gaze will catch / and the knowing between them is old and wise / as the quiet hum of hills / Just think / the newly born / deprived of this / Fuck Nestlé forever

Fuck / *Kipling*

If I'd been there when he wrote / The White Man's Burden / If I'd seen the / half devil half child / line form in him / If in reaching for his neck I tipped his inkwell / If gallons spilled / like Black blood / across the middle passage / If we fell into it and washed up back on gold coast shores / I would spur him inland at gunpoint / find a village in which it's practised / Force Kipling to watch the punishment unfold / where / forsaking execution or confinement / after wrong-doings / the guilty is stood in a large circle before every man woman and child / who recount tales of the guilty's good deeds and kindness / Two days this lasts before the circle is broken / to celebration / and the accused welcomed back to the tribe / Then I'll lean to whisper in Kipling's ear / before flicking the eager trigger / Such kindness is what we devil child do / and our shit is too good for you

Fuck / *Red Bull*

So / When I first came to this country ten years ago / one of my boys told me / Come to a club / one woman there likes you / I said / Really / Is she Black or White / He refused to tell me / said I was racist / So I go / music is loud / people dancing / my friend points out one White girl / I greet her and I didn't know she's been watching me for ages / She orders my favourite drink / two cans of Red Bull / I'm Muslim / I don't drink / I wanted to pay and you know what / She said / No No No / She will buy the drinks / I said / Wow / It's never happened before / woman pay for my shit / I'm loving this / It was time to go / she ask where I live / Five minutes down the road / She said / Let's buy drinks on the way / and paid as well / My friends I was impressed / You wonder why they say White people are mean and I started changing myself you know / So she ask / Am I going out the next day / I say / I'm not / We got home / Finish eating / shag / two / three / times / You know what they call me / Mr Lover Lover / Around eight in the morning / this Jamaican girl I met when I was doing security called me / Where are you / and I like that Jamaican girl well well / I been wanting her for ages / I said / I'm home / She said / Can we meet / Come to Walworth Road / So I sent a text message to my friend to act as if he just landed / at Gatwick Airport / so I'll come pick him up / I put the phone on loudspeaker / ARE YOU IN GATWICK NOW / He said / AHHH YEAH YEAH / and the White girl started looking at me / I said / Babes / Babes / I have to pick up my friend at the airport / You know how it is Babes / And you know what she said to me / You know what she said to me / She said / I thought you weren't going out / That's why I never trust Black people / Believe you me she said that / I was feeling a little guilty / but after that / I didn't care / No way I'll let the Black girl down / See Whites don't like us / Am I wrong

Fuck / *The Incalculable Unknown*

For Rambisayi & Panashe

Whomsoever asks if Black folk can be racist / I will now answer
/ One / Define racism / Two / Define Black / Three / In which
world are these Black folk Black / Four / To whom is the racism
aimed / Five / Recount their history with said group / Six / In
what context is the question raised / Seven / Who are you who
asks / and should all answers satisfy / should they intersect / as
in a Venn diagram / the lines in praxis / spiralling toward an
outlined emptiness / an incalculable unknown / a power vacuum
in which humanity is equal / an Earth I've never known / one un-
obliterated by Whiteness / For the souls of Black folk swallowed
by ocean water / For the ancestors whipped to string meat and
screams / For the boys handcuffed for breathing / who leave
precincts in body bags / For the dark girls chemically cooking out
their melanin / bleaching / their brown eyes blue and blind / the
best I could venture / would be / maybe / maybe / Fuck that / No

Fuck / *White Saviour Complex*

Her name is Jane or Amber / She will have the best intentions / She will have the petal of this reason for a tongue / She will have been five / The glow off the National Geographic will have bathed her face golden / She will have paused on the dark child's swollen belly / thin limbs / ribs / the flies / She will have slipped off her big sister's Louboutins / skipped the play room / through her mother's walk-in wardrobe / to the pool / to ask if the child could attend supper / Her mother's laugh will shimmer her diamonds / She will explain / The world is the world / Some work hard / like your father / forging oil contracts / Some just don't / But we are still to help the poor in Africa / She will have wanted to ever since / Her utmost sincerity will cut you to silence / She will bloom anew

Fuck / *Tiffany*

Men in Black / Part 1 / Will Smith ducks into a shooting range / The targets are cardboard cutouts on zip wires / hurtling through strobe lights / sirens / smoke / Will calmly shoots / once / into the ghoulish darkness / When Zed / the invigilator asks / What the hell happened / pulling up Tiffany / a cardboard blonde / with Will's bullet through her head / Will explains the first monster / dangling off a streetlight / is just working out / another / snarling / for the tissue in its hand / is actually sneezing / but that eight-year-old blonde / amongst them / clutching a book on Quantum Physics / seemed / the most out of place / the one suspicious / the one / alien / to that cardboard ghetto / Should my daughter ever walk / the world's corners alone / I'd want her confidence to be as that White girl's / to believe trained men will clear monsters from her path / Should I have been taken for a monster at night / a bullet through me / from the trained / yet less discerning / should she then need warning of the world's true colours / Will should tell my daughter / he should be the one

Fuck / *Aneurysms*

My father tried to walk again / which is to say / after half his brain went dark / he wished one synapse back to life / he urged a firefly from an abyss / he willed a spark from swamp / he sought glow-worms from marshland / he stirred lightning bugs from graves / he carved sparkplugs from networks of drowned matter / he tried to jumpstart a galaxy /

My father conducts lights to order / which is to say / a symphony of stars align for each step / which is to say / walking / which is to say / miracle

Fuck / *Love*

I want to tell my twin sister I love her but what I really mean is her arm around my waist when we were half-formed halflings in mother's womb is the closest I've ever been to God / I want to tell my mother I love her but mean I want to spoon the arthritis out of her swollen knuckles and kiss them back to nimble freedom / I want to tell my father I love him but mean will I ever crown him with the comfort he deserves / I want to tell my nephews I love them but mean some shadows seethe for Black skin and I want to shield them from its falling / I want to tell my people I love them but mean I want them to have thrived on an uncarved continent / I want to tell my lover I love her but mean her hug is palatial divinity / is my father's crowning comfort / my mother's dancing hands / my nephews' careless wandering / is uncharted territory / wild as it is pure / What is / to love / when all your meanings are ineffable sufferings / What is it to mean more than you can / Who else carries half hugs in inflamed hands empty of comforts full of shadows and ancient aching acres

Fuck / *Diminutives*

In one dream we are horses / our tails are dark blue flames / our hooves are coal half-crushed to diamonds / The racecourse is obstacled with glass ceilings / slow squad cars and niggling doubt / Our task is to reach the end with our selves / our names intact / In the stands the loud-mouthed / the well-meaning / mix with / the downtrodden / the vicious / All have failed to master the tongue's soft curl / They call us daft approximations / teeth flashing / each like a dagger in the night / each syllable a fresh cut / each cut a blood bath / Our mothers who are tied / strain at their reins / They prance and dance for us and burst into flames

Fuck / *Trees*

Dego / Though we know it isn't his birth name / Dego he is to us / his scattered swiftness / calling for the dull red orb / It is dusk and behind him / we don't know their names either / but they line the ball court / claw up through the concrete to hold him to their thin shadows / Dego jumps higher / arms outstretched to suggest a safe pass / be more visible / but is a Christ-shaped silhouette against their darkness / as if nailed to wood / strangled in their grip / the way we've been strangled before / strange fruit framed by air / dangling / How many crossed over here / who else shuffled earth / attempted flight / and lost it all among the trees

Fuck / *Dante*

The day Melissa complained I spent too much time dribbling and I better assess my priorities or else / Dante stepped on the court with a fake left and release so crisp / it looked like a nine o'clock / you could set your watch by it / Dante said he wanted dudes to know what time it is / which was a hip hop reference drawled in his thick Brooklyn accent / which was all we needed to follow him like lemmings / through the estate / up to the roof where he'd look into the middle distance over our listening city / at the few drifting clouds / clumped together like we were around him / and say something stupid like / You can tell what kind of Dad you'll be by how you play the game / how you screen against danger so your boy can fly / and if you ain't there his world comes crashing down / Jamie goes quiet like he does after losing a game / shivering like he badly needs a hug but the sky is just too vast to hold him / like a man / Roger asks suddenly how Dante got so tall / Jamie says / That's a stupid question / Dante says / Not at all / he just copied Jordan / spent one summer hanging from monkey bars with weights / around his ankles till his bones drew out / Last time I saw Melissa / I had bricks tied around my feet / dangling from the crossbar of a metal swing as she sucked Dante's bottom lip beneath the street light / which flickered once / twice / then finally guttered out

Fuck / *Dystopian Loneliness*

There are nights when I'm streets deep / lost / forging new footpaths through a city / It feels like I'm the only soul alive / I look up at towers / blocks / so shadowed / they are looming omens / Then dawn comes / throwing its soft wide fists against the overwhelming darkness / igniting its cold urban bones / kindling its clockwork machinery to roaring life / slowly glowing up the world / Being with you feels like that

Fuck / *Fate*

And instead of chicken claw / spliced hooves or gnarled roots / my hands looked smooth as psalms / as quiet poems / I held yours and claiming myself a palm reader / pushed down flattening the flesh mounds / I ran my tongue along your lifelines / gasping I could not fathom their darkness / your obscured future / its uncharted rivers and thin seas / so purple-brown / so bleak as space / I feared its void and prayed / into its nakedness for light / for us / let there be light

Fuck / *Bikram's Yoga*

Sometimes friendship means agreeing / Yes / You were right to cheat / Your Bikram-Yoga boyfriend / all that hot air rising / believed the hubris of his purity / folded his students down to Sasangasana and pushed in / his sense of worth so dizzyingly high / he forgot the murky concrete of his soul / much like Paris clings to its old romance / All Namaste means is Hello anyway / You were right / You sashayed out his performative life / You didn't say goodbye

Fuck / *Concrete*

The bus will ride through the city / The rain clouds will gather / The trials of urban light will fail / Water will claim victory / The valleys we have sculpted / the hills we have built / the tall lean structures / all will shift / The sediments of who we once were / the haggard seeds we have been / the hidden down-trodden parts / which turn and mulch beneath / will break through our stone facades / And should we sigh at what surfaces and think / This bitter earth what fruit it bears / let us rejoice that there is feast / Such bountiful sorrow

Fuck / *Logophobia*

So / Things we don't have words for in our language don't exist /
I have an autistic niece / low on the spectrum / you wouldn't tell
by looking at her / but last week / my sister called / crying / said
/ I can't handle it anymore / Can't handle it / I said / What's the
matter / What's going on / She said / We went to braid our hair
in a Ghanaian salon and she threw a tantrum / The place was
packed / Saturday / all African clientele / started looking at her
/ shouting / Deal with your child / you are spoiling this child /
Before / I told her / It's common / don't be shy / just tell people
this child is autistic / She did and all hell broke loose / They were
shouting / It's your fault / You are the cause of this / Just because
she said it / They told her / Slap the autism out of her / slap it out
/ I wanted to get involved to help / but the aunties tell me / What
do I know of raising children / My hands are tied / I'm just a man
/ Am I wrong

Fuck / *Paris*

Jean Paul / arriving at the mouth of the evening / stands in the R&B club doorway / its soupy darkness framing him like a parched white tongue / and that Black body funk / that moist want / for a lover's kiss to touch a broken back / like a firefly dappling Mississippi swamp / is the singer's voice over baselines / Its want for comfort / its wailing for warmth / a language / a meaning Jean Paul's being can't fathom / so squeezes past him / like cries for freedom / into the bourgeois night

Fuck / *Swamps*

#After Jennifer Givhan

I carry them into the water / I carry choir hymns and calls to prayer / I carry the body impaled / I carry its bleeding / I carry the moon the star and the black stone / I carry the pastor's wandering hands and the Imam's stiff visits / I carry the burning flesh and headless bodies / I carry dusk's grass-blade tongue / I carry the curtained whispering / I carry the smoking history / I carry my father's confusion and mother's shame / I carry my father's shame and mother's confusion / I rub them together / They burst into flames / I carry Abraham and Ibrahim / I carry the slaughtered lamb's scorched carcass / I lift the sacrificial off the soil / I carry the eagle's wing and horses' hooves / I carry the whole coat of arms / the black shield aloft like a coffin / I carry them to the swamp / I drag them back into their waters / I drown them in darkness and slice them out

Fuck / *Boys*

It starts early / A man compliments the tight nut of his grandson's fist / Hit Me / he says / holding open his palms / The boy strikes and winces / The man says / Shake it off / We are men / We feel nothing / The boy tucks the tiny fracture into the sleeve of himself and strikes again / The fracture burrows deeper / Over the years others join / This when older boys squash butterflies / This when the teacher ridicules his painting / This when the fairy's light dims in the film / They swarm inward / a shoal of needles through meat / shredding the vicissitudes of himself / At twenty they are a nest of thorns around his heart / They flatten to a hard shell / They close and crush him in / At thirty he is imprisoned for a fight he can't justify / His heart is a gnarled knuckle now / but holds a spot of light / thin as spiritskin / in which the boy he was and the man he could have been / whisper / in hushed starlight / in dimmed symphonies / of other ways of being

Fuck / *Sunflowers*

What I'm trying to say is / Kelechi hates sunflowers / because Tyrone grew obsessed / after his class daytripped to the countryside / That first time he left the hulking concrete of his ends / that afternoon where the sky / enormous as it always is / looked down on him / Tyrone / for the first time / looked back / as if into the face of God / properly studying its swoops and tonalities / the contours of the countries of clouds / and the force that rose in him to match its unblinking vastness / brought him down to his knees where he squelched his fingers into the good and clean earth / drilling his black thumb into the blacker soil / The teacher scolded him all they way home / for his mud-streaked seat and soiled trousers / What she didn't know is Tyrone had planted saplings of his spirit / among the fields of barley / and seeds of himself among the sunflowers / and these kept calling for him when they returned to the city of bricks / clawing for their kin / Though he filled his room with them / he couldn't match life out in the fields / the sky's unencumbered gaze over their choir of black faces / their petals like flattened crowns or ruffled haloes / So Tyrone walked out his fourth floor window to join them / and Tyrone never came home

Fuck / *Symphonies*

#After Beethoven
For Zahzee

Months from now it will happen again / in gin-and-juice loose-tongued-stupor / I'll be like fuck classical music / fuck those elitist dudes in darks suits / There's nothing I haven't seen J Dilla do / that dude with a MIDI and a Mac / composed the whole world right on wax / and I will forget

this analogue afternoon / the radio's dial snagging a whole sunrise / or what one must certainly sound like / Earth glowing up awake / coming into its own bloom of airwaves / of warmth and amber / of booming horizons / horn / bassoon and oboes / tugging the dawn's ochre aura over leafy-headed forests / down noble brows of bush / brave bark / soft moss and root / to subterranean bedrock of bones and blues / and threading through this / a piano line / like a girl reborn as bird / her bright persistent spirit / flitting with the flute's lilting limber / I reached to spin that radio's dial but she had got to me / had me hooked in / to the orchestra / the symphony / the pit / with its wise wood and windy ways / the oak and gold / the whole world of her held me in its holy mouth / in its halting time / had me lifted / from the tight urban gloom / into a light filled with room / into a room filled with light

Fuck / *Light*

For James

The ice-like clarity Inuits enjoy / of their native skies / the way it gathers the natural soft / of snow-reflected light / into its wide self / holds it up to frame stars / long after rays retire / isn't cherished or sought out by us / urban-dwelling folk / who carved our own stars from glass / sowed in them electric seeds / steel nuclei to burn / granting us effervescent luminescence / This egg-sized supernova / caged by lampshade / I choose to free now / I flick the switch / draw closed the blinds / unplug the artificial for a miner's light / a lone candle / flame blinking in the dark / and search my native self / for anything shimmering

Fuck / *Time*

Once upon a time / Yo-Yo Ma / traveling through Botswana searching for music / finds a local shaman singing / into the savannah / He rushes to notate the melody / Please sing again / he requests / to which the shaman sings something else and explains / to the baffled Yo-Yo Ma / that earlier / clouds had covered the sun and wild antelope grazed in the distance / But the dial of the world had twirled since / The antelopes had cantered into some other future / The clouds had gone / so the song had to change / had to slough off the chains us mortals clasp everything with / even our fluid wrists / The universe in fact is monstrously indifferent to the presence of man / We are small as moth wing fall / in an orchestra broad as galaxies / playing a symphony Time isn't bothered to fathom / It respects no constant and is always moving on

Fuck / *Drums*

When I claim hip hop as afrofuturist expressionism / Exhibit A is the ancient West African Sankofa symbol / of a bird walking forward whilst looking back / like a rapper following a beat's forward progression / whilst recalling lyrics / anticipating the future whilst conjuring the past / and the rapper is the gasp of stillness between / the ghost in the time machine / Say time is marked by drums / and each strike stakes its signature / The rapper's task is to find within its solid lines / equilibrium / to fuck up the drum's ubiquitous significance by rhyming / on / within / or off its beat / to render it inaudible / invisible / fluid as if a bird dancing through a stave of barbed wires / its wings aflutter / like a tongue between gritted teeth / twirling urban narratives into timeless myth / shit / it's the stuff of science fiction / ain't it / each rapper's mouth a Quantum realm / a Tardis / a Delorean / and the beat maker a mad scientist / Y'all don't see how all electricity is Sango's lightning pulse / that Dr Emmet Brown is Grand Master Flash in disguise / that Andre 3000 is the greatest Time Lord / who grabbed a mic / to spit

Fuck / *Our Future*

When our scorching planet ignites the last evacuating airship to cook its soft cargo of human flesh in an expanding fireball and fragments of its propeller blades thunk inches deep into tree trunks in the straggling forest beneath / What I want to know is which will survive / which strain / which wood grain will hold encoded / like a fingerprint pushed into wet clay / that final day of reckoning when this cerulean blue ordained world we have corroded a toxic grey / begins its self-reclamation starting with that tree / a lone lieutenant / a desperate sentinel / erect / through the falling ball of fire / jet fuel and smouldering meat / its face of leaves weighed with dust / its waist of branches noosed in plastic bags / yet standing stubborn in its shaggy majesty / amidst the ship's carnage / like a righteous middle finger thrust at all humanity / proud in the snarling sky

Fuck / *Humanity*

Fuck Humanity I want to bellow / like a card-carrying champion of the Nihilist Society / fuck all the ways even our most earnest faithful / folded over / humbled deep down considered attempts / at amending our venomous ills / undoes itself / think / almond milk and California wildfires / nitrogen fertiliser and industrial food waste / factory emission limits and the trade in carbon offsets / free market and exploitation / voluntary work and White saviour complex / vegan avocado diets and deforestation / phones to connect our lonely spirits and Black bodies in coltan mines / Fuck every single attempt / Our best bet is to annihilate our vicious selves / I want to bellow / as Ellie pushes her three-year-old hand into the calloused cave of mine / Her fingers / frail as elderberry petals / flutter / She calls me down to the careful constellations blooming / in the brown universe / of her brimming eyes and all I am folds over / humbled deep down / reconsidering attempts / at amending our venomous ills / even if it undoes me

Fuck / *Factory Emissions*

The thing about fireflies / these winged soft-bodied beautiful beetles / commonly called lightning bugs / that produce a cold light / low on ultraviolet frequencies / is that their lower abdomens glow green or pale red / Sometimes it is their larvae that emits light / like the kindling of a rebel's spirit before flaring in adulthood / Their wings are leathery / yet leaf-like / and adolescent bugs are quick to fly / like a teen to the open road / tail lights trailing in the sky's highway

Far above / factory emissions condense / to sulphur nitrogen oxide / commonly called acid rain / This will singe through tail lights / eat through wings / to make flightpaths lopsided / loose / like a teen driver / careening through traffic / tires melting / fated to die

Fuck / *Conferences*

#After Emily Johnson

Have I told you of the oak / that grew where we are now / that you can find in aerial shots of the city / going back sixty years / before it was slashed down for this conference centre / which would fit within it / so wide was its trunk / I was thinking how flimsy my limbs would seem held against its slimmest branch / I looked up to check its wondrous penumbra of leaves and saw instead the cast-iron beams of the ceiling / and not the sky I had seen earlier this morning / outside / when I noticed again how impossible it is to fully grasp / such clear and present borderlessness / in which a sparrow hawk swooped / and above it flew an airplane / and though I knew the plane was thousands of feet further up / I stood there / just in case / the hawk needed me to catch / my fingers laced into a fleshy ready nest / my breath trapped / my chest clenched / my shuddering shuddering heart / and I was that sky / our bird / this tree / these leaves / the building / you / and me

Fuck / *History*

For the early years I spent skimming the half desert / half battlefields in Northern Nigeria / I wonder if the ground misses me / If in the fallow shadowy holes I'd hide / giggling at my searching sisters / my toe prints are still held by the dust / What if my ancestors were the dust / Which Fulani conquest spilled their blood / In which setting did they find romance / What if it is their meeting in me that spurs grains of sand to taste like sparks off clashing swords / like seeds of stars or moon nucleus / Sometimes I dream in Hausa and have no idea what is being said / Sometimes Arabic calligraphy looks to me like flowers on fire / What if the Quran is a pressed forest of burning trees / Is the call to prayer a line of low flames / What is it to miss a way of being I was too young to be / The largest possible quantity of anything is a lifetime / When my father returned from Hajj doubting Islam / I was asleep / When the Imam's thug aimed an AK at our car / I still believed / until I stared down the barrel and saw no light at the tunnel's end / So began a lifetime of questions / each page a desert / each thin blue line a cold horizon / all the waiting words are shards of parched stars / the looming stanzas like rising moons / an infinite infidel hiding in me

Fuck / *Nigeria*

#After Fatimah Asghar

You are Nigerian until they massacre your elders / until the breeze blows thick with blood / You are defiant until they erase your home / burn your harvests / shred your clothes / until the locals forget you built the road you walked in on / You disbelieve until they separate your husband from his head / your wife from her eyes / your brother from his belly / until your sister's drool thickens the dust / and no limb stirs when your child is called / You are infidel until your parents ask you to leave / to pack a handkerchief with food and run / You are a refugee until the river spits you out / until the miles of woods and wilds of pastures stop clawing at your raw skin / You are brave until bullets and mosquitos bite the night the same way / until bombs fall frequent as fruit / until any whistling empties your bladder / You are a wreck until the guns dance to silence / until your people fold / officially surrender / You are relieved until night sweats / trembling / the swollen bellies of skeletal children begin haunting your every dream / For the scorched skin stretched across skulls and their looming eyes in your quiet hours / you are Biafran until you die / until the struggle breaks your back

Fuck / *Boko Haram*

After the guns had danced to silence / the boy whose father was
killed / joined the others / sipping cough syrup / in the tight
corners of the parched village / their eyes hollow and hungry
/ for things their widowed mothers could not provide / There
were never enough schools to teach / the possible rift between
thought and action / The boys would lash out / wild as scuffling
dogs / in the scavenging heat / which the men who killed their
fathers took / for killer instincts / and came back masked / in the
Quran's floral lilt / promising their empty bellies fulfilment / their
empty hands purpose / empty lives love / The boys followed their
lulling tongues / into the desert / days and nights / tottering past
rattlesnakes and scorpions / as the prophet Muhammed / peace
be upon him / had done / seeking his destiny / in caves / where
more stories of him were flattened / like curved knives and slipped
/ like drips of concrete / into the broken parts of the breaking boys
/ Bit by bone by brick / they were built into the militia of black
flags and fire / who return to the village now / guns dancing /
who speak into the silence / over the fresh corpses / to the newly
hungry and hollow-eyed boys / promising fulfilment / purpose /
love / their mouths like gardens / blooming in the desert's bleak

Fuck / *Deserts*

#After Kayo Chingonyi

Take the path that begins among the neem trees / as far as the stream bled of all water / Sift through its dry bed of discarded boots / You will find a rust-covered compass / Buff against your sleeve / When it winks with sunlight / go whichever way its needle points north / Turn right where the farmland thins to a grassy sheen / You will come to a village with none of its youth / Place your palm on the closest hot hut's husk / until you sense the wind's quickening tremble the walls / Punch through / Push down into the hole and grab the topmost sash of vulture feathers / Hold one between your teeth until your tongue numbs / Bite down / When you regain consciousness / The huts will be the sand dunes around you / The desert will hold you in its golden nothing / Lift the camel skull by your inner left thigh / Look through where once lived its left eye / You will find / stretched from horizon to the petrified sky / the answer to who you were meant to be / how you bested that self / and why this is still just you / beginning

Fuck / *Camels*

Found poem /

So / there were two rivals / one tough lawman and a legendary smuggler / Throughout their careers / they had been fighting each other / from job to job / post to post / their paths always crossed / One day that lawman was stationed at a border-crossing this smuggler had to pass / to reach the next country / The lawman started rubbing his hands / I will catch him today / He won't escape / When the smuggler arrived / he shouted / Climb down from that camel / Now / He searched everything / every pocket / didn't find anything / so he had to let him cross / Next month / same thing / Get off that camel / Searched everything / held the smuggler in blazing heat for hours / no water / no shade / found nothing / had to let him go / Third time / the lawman checked the camel's mouth / strip-searched the man on the road there / stood him naked / even shined a torchlight up his nyash / Didn't find anything / Lawman said / I know you are smuggling something / Smuggler said / You found nothing / have to let me go / so he did / Years later / when they had retired / Lawman / standing outside his house / saw the old smuggler / inviting him for a cup of tea / he said / All those years coming and going on those dusty camels / I searched everything / even you / found nothing / But you were smuggling something / What was it / Smuggler laughed / All these years you didn't know / Lawman said / What was it / Tell me / You know what he said / Camels / Incredible story / Am I wrong

Fuck / *Dust*

Have you exploded awake / at the 4am forge of darkest night / to your heart's brutish beating / and to calm the raging bull of it / tried focusing on anything / the nearest pencil's nascent point / a famished sunflower's slump / scrunched-up tissue like a second-hand cloud / Did you flick the lamp's switch / notice a thin film of dust across the tabletop / move to wipe it clean / but freeze / recalling a half-read article / which your Googling confirms / Household dust is 80% human skin / So you lean in to inspect each speck / Which was part eyelid / Which was parched lip / Which was once ear and listened in / You consider surveying your entire house / brush and pan in hand / to sweep into a bowl / all you have been / to hold it like cereal at breakfast / and spoon yourself back into you / to gift to you / you / but first run a finger across that tabletop and bring what you find / close enough to smell / close enough to lick

Fuck / *Carrots*

Friday night / barber shop / it's starting again / Samuel / his hand poised over Ethan's head / is Basquiat before an uncrowned king / is Henry Moore before a block of wood / is Sigmund Freud before a mass of contradictions / Clippers / paintbrush / chisel / voice / the task is the same / to bring to light what lies within

The shop is stock full of us / our skin all the tints and tones of wood / our heads of wild foliage

Kwame / just taxied from Saudi Arabia / slides off his cap / says his driver was a woman / how progressive London is / compared to Saudi which banned them from driving / Why / Ethan asks / wide-eyed beneath Samuel / Because / Kwame says / Fear of infidelity / They even banned courgettes / Cucumbers are illegal

Emmanuel who knows where this is going / he / who owns the shop / who's heard all types of talk / sighs into his client's head

Why / Ethan asks / Because of self-pleasure / Winston cackles from the centre of the shop / Because of vegetables they won't need a man / What about carrots / asks Uncle Sizwe / Ah too pointy

/ Kwame responds / But you can carve them / pipes Hammed from the back / They can be huge / Yes size matters / and the tide of conversation swells among the men / some as if captains sway in their seats / others stand up / out on a limb begging / for the sanity and sanctity of sex / covering their son's ears / risible in the ridicule

A passerby peeking might wander what it is / If something's in the water / some loosening opiate / a dark tonic / Black juice we have drunk / what magic is this welding / of loose-necked Pinocchios / gym freaks / thin-limbed / immigrants / emigrants / fantastic fools / fathers / sons / rulers and the ruled / loud in our laughter / silent in our suffering / what is this binding / what is set free

All I know is Ethan's cut is clean / Samuel released what lay within / his mass trimmed / the wood gleams / and though he is one of us / now he is crowned king

Fuck / *The Joker*

When Jack Nicholson was informed of Heath Ledger's death / after playing the Joker / Jack dragged from his cigarette / shrugged and said / I warned him / I want to believe should my elders ever warn / of the lithe and lovely lure of the incalculable unknown yet dangerous certain / the boy who is easy spooked by night breeze / the one whose blood curdles at foggy shuffles / he / who I've always been / I want to believe he would shimmy out the whole in which I've tried to bury him / to lay at the bruised altar by the seat of my soul / a primal scream as if a burning sacrifice / that I might wake me / the fuck up / enough to sidestep foolish machismo / and save my only self

Fuck / *Batman*

The promise was / should one fall into a cave of bats / should one be engulfed by hundreds of beating wings / should one be beaten / scratched or bitten / one would emerge / half-human half-invincible / enough to sharpen fear down to a tight-toothed weapon / with which to gnaw the criminal urban underworld / down to pulpy nothings / protecting us all / The promise was / should an animal's essence seep into a child / knowing what damage loose power brews / he would accept himself as host / his body a fleshy petri dish / to guide its mutation to goodness / Instead the promise / turned ravenous / leapt from host to host / country to country / blood to blood / its million teeth chewing through our simple lungs / We closed down our offices / it hung on our clothes / We fled from cities / it clung to our cars / We stayed in bed / it came for our dreams / a curdled crown / a rank coronation / a crude corroding of our inner sanctums / our public spaces / our minute planning / our mapped-out futures / horoscopes and forecasts / the dark parts of star charts / all emptied out / to an assiduous stillness / the promise gorging on our numbed lives / our startled terror / And when the promise retreated / it left its fangs in the sky / its claws in our pockets / its foul breath huffed between us in shopping lines / its warning to return should we cease vigilance / to claim more from the survived

Fuck / *Foggy Shuffles*

Because the learner driver is stalled in the middle lane / the mackerel's fin caught in the net / the student 50% sure of the answer / the sunflower root a finger's width from water / Because the high heel is caught in the metal grate / and the blind rat's nose is clogged by fog / I believe the Devil we know / is the work of a Biblical hype man / an MC who strayed far beyond the call / of duty / into the fantastic / conjuring Beelzebub as a hulking goat / a crimson winged demon / a fire-breathing blood sucker / not how he truly appears / coyly / quiet / a flat-capped smiler / of small thumbs and soft words / who comes with options / shuffling through hunkered fog / offering to trade gifts so slight / they feel like a right already earned / clear nasal cavities / a thinner heel / thimbles of water / half a percent more / one smaller fin / and all the time in the world

Fuck / *Empire*

Fuck / *Empire* was commissioned by the Manchester Literature Festival and Museum of Manchester in response to an artefact / a sacred royal ceremonial tusk / one of thousands of such items / stolen by British soldiers from the Kingdom on Benin in 1897

1/

1840 / This was the year the British Empire snuck thirty thousand chests / of purest opium across the Chinese border / When the twelve million they had hooked on the drug / so decimated their brittle lives / shrinking to ghoulish spectres of thin skin / the Emperor saw beyond his own greed / to crack down on the drug he had already made illegal / When he refused whatever bribe the crown had offered / turning down the White men who came cloaked in darkness / preferring the health of his people / over the wealth of their world / when he refused them / stuffing the white powder / down the nostrils of the sleepy string of villages / that bejewelled the borders of his country / the Empire attacked / musket fire rattling the hills / valleys and bones of clouds / mowing the Chinese soldiers down among the thickets of bush / their bellies scattered open / such that the clear streams of melting snow / ran red with blood / Whether or not the British soldiers danced in their blood is unconfirmed / but what I know is bloody bootprints were found / from India to Nigeria / in shrines and holy places / from mines to precious spaces where kings meet / the paths and patterns of violence playing out / across the world

2/

1884 / This was the year the British Empire sunk thirty thousand troops into Africa / clawing for its land / thirsty for its rivers / famished for its flesh / When the Berlin conference that year / so decimated any false pretence / of development / humanity or basic respect / the Empire demanded monopoly over trade / along the broad Benin River / When the governor refused / turning down the White men who came with hearts of darkness / rebutting their watery offers / convincing local chiefs to follow suit / preferring the health of his people over the wealth of their world / the Empire attacked / warships sailing up river / Maxim guns and cannon fire shuddering the shores / inlets and shallow pools / crashing through the governor's war boys along the banks of the river / bursting open their bellies / their crushed skulls / such that the water grew thick with bodies / thickening with blood / Whether or not the British soldiers danced in their blood is unconfirmed / but what I know is bloody bootprints were found / down river / inland / in the clearing where the chiefs gathered to meet / the paths and patterns of violence playing out / across the land

3/

1896 / This was the year the British Empire snuck three hundred men up river / into the forest / towards Benin City / After the snatching into slavery of millions of men and women / so decimated the beautiful city / reducing its precolonial majesty / to a clutch of tattered huts / The King / the Oba of Benin / banned trade with whichever White men came looking / letting local chiefs know / the vehemence of their unwelcome / They came regardless / soldiers disguised as merchants / again cloaked in darkness / the forest gloom thick on their necks / their hunger for Black flesh / for Black wealth / like a self-imposed curse around them / The King / preferring the mental health of his people / over the wealth of the world / attacked / the spears and shields of his men rattling the soil / leaves and canopies of the forest / mowing the British down among the mounds of hot mud and foliage / such that only two survived to tell the tale / Whether or not the King's men danced in their blood is unconfirmed / but what I know is the story that was told / so roused a vengeance in the heart of Empire / they would return to the forest / hands loaded with flames

4/

1897 / This was the year the Empire struck / There were boys play-fighting in the soft grass / girls with half-braided hair snoozing beside their mothers / There were infants trying to catch flies idling by in the heavy heat / fathers working the wide fields / young men distracted among them / watching young women drawing water from wells / all immersed in the glowing minutiae of their lives / all ripe with laughter / their lips plump with love / All must have turned towards a trumpet's sound / all must have gathered / excited at the spectacle of marching soldiers / spectacular in their red coats / curious to the kids / who didn't know their strange oaths / didn't know their intentions / Did toddlers count their silver buttons / gleaming like flat stars / Who stopped smiling first / when the volley of musket fire rang / Who was sprayed with blood / Who smelt the gunpowder / When the others turned / scattering into city / screaming through its streets / as the soldiers gave chase / Who was too shocked to move / When the Empire came to crush the kingdom / to turn its town and villages to ash / to hang the king wherever he was captured / when they touched their hands to the walls of the city / wrapping its clay in flames / who stood by / Who could watch the world burn

5/

1898 / This was the year the tusk entered the Empire / When the soldier who smuggled it across the ocean / strapped to the ship's creaking hull / tells how it came into his possession / his tongue will swell with heroism / his throat thick with valour / He won't mention his spine / shuddering as Benin City burned / that he watched infants suffocate / that whole families died clinging to each other / clawing the smoke for air / that flames he had lit licked the sky / turning the night to day / that when the looting began / he crashed into the King's palace / and stood / stupefied by its majesty / that in the throne room / he felt spirits of past kings weighing heavy on him / that they sized up his soul and found its honour lacking / that this shamed him / that he shamed himself / that the elephant tusk gleamed as if conscious of its royalty / that his hand shook as he reached to touch the figures and inscription carved in its curve / that he sensed a century of history beneath his fingers / that he knew he was unworthy to touch / so torched the palace as he left / dragging his plunder / that he could not bear its weight to the ship / or from the ship to the shore / or from the shore to his home / so dragged it again / through the streets of Salford and Manchester / with fragments of ivory / breaking against the cobbled stones / splintering into snow

6/

1903 / This was the year the elephants struck the Empire / Because they do not forget / because they are the whales of their world / custodians of its land / forefathers of forefathers / who sat with kings / who wore ancient history like living skin / from the world beyond / they watched news / wild as the fire that ate Benin City / spread / heard tongues wagging salacious with stolen riches / saw that those who had plundered their kingdom / who turned its palace to ash / carried three thousand other items across the ocean / to hawk to the highest bidders / These thieves greased their hands / with sacramental benches / ceremonial masks / stone necklaces / bronze plaques / ivory pendants / envious of what art their tusks could hold / these parts of their bodies / indeed their very bones / to trade / to display / in Monday meeting rooms / to bury in cellars / to hide in sheds / to leave in toy chests / to poke and prod like curiosities / evidence of a land of cannibals / a world of the weird / They were dissected / mishandled / misrepresented / mislabelled / misused / misremembered and forgotten / The elephants came like frost settling on cities / their fragments of bone like talismans / drawing them from the world of spirits / asking they march again / They came like fog in the night / like clouds of conscience / like continents of questions / and swarmed into the spaces where men bury answers / and began to push them out

7/

1914 / This was the year the palace was rebuilt / when survivors of the burned Benin City returned to its carcass / still crushed / still scarred / still touched with flames / They came picking through its scorched fields and crumbling courtyards / gathering fragments of ivory / fistfuls of brittle jewels from the ruins / piecing back memories of what was lost / Mothers spoke of their fallen infants / Soldiers of their fallen men / Young wives of their missing husbands / All about their friends / Some sat on the naked soil / trying to root themselves in their ancestral past / raising the dead in song / Some swayed in dance / their bodies like smoke / like sweat / like greased bones / cleaving the air in two / clawing at themselves / Some cried into the parched fields / their tears salting the earth / The new king wanted to speak of passed dynasties / of how the British Empire had sunk its claws deeper into the land / had lined its borders with blood / had formed Nigeria / into a factory / to further steal from its people / but said nothing / for the crown had officers / posted / watching / He waited for the wise ones / at the old clearing / who whispered about empires / as dusk took the sky / that such is their destiny / to crumble and fall / and even their powerful enemies / time would consume them all

Fuck / *You*

My love / I promised / should you ever say / You are not a body that has a soul / But a soul that has a body / And that body is within the soul / I'd respond / Fuck you / Fuck outta here with that New Age shit / but I haven't / because early this week / crawling between the crisp sheets for an afternoon nap / I fell back / expecting the goose feather pillow to gather my loose neck / but instead / kept falling / as if the feathers had parted / into the smoothest clouds / then just-forming snow / then hard rain / then red mist / then fire raging fire / then molten stone / oh boiling earth / oh liquid metal / oh solid thunder / oh fire / all fury / through which I kept tumbling / then all went silent / as if I'd fallen off the cliff edge of quiet / into space / all blue / all black / all blinking its many mooned and millioned mysteries / all of them ministering to me / and amongst them was I / drifting / at the slowest speed possible / yet far above / out and wide / as the planet's girth / all expanding / all still / all me / still there / in that bed / moon-wrecked between its sheets / gasping and grasping at it / For all the fleshy sparkle of the body's glow / for all its muscular mystery / how could it contain all I had seen / all I had been / unless its reach is beyond itself / further than its bones allow / unless a soul / is beyond its body / its edges blurring to brilliant madness

ACKNOWLEDGEMENTS

Thanks to Tobi Kyeremateng and Apples and Snakes for inviting me to read the first ever Fuck / Poem at the live poetry event Jawdance. Without her enthusiasm and that safe space to share, this book would not exist.

Thanks to editors at the following publications where some Fuck / Poems were published in earlier versions: *Aleph Review*, *Ambit*, *Friction*, *Magma*, *Perverse Magazine*, *POETRY*, *Poetry Review*, *Wildness*.

Thanks to Nii Ayikwei-Parkes, Nathalie Teitler and Tom Chivers for their constant encouragement and support.

Thanks to Inua Ellams Snr, Veronica Ellams, Fatima Ellams, Mariam Asuquo, Hadiza Alex-Ellams, Wayne Holloway Smith, Theresa Lola, Theresa Ikoko, Krystle Lai, Rambisayi Marufu, Panashe Chigumadzi, Anish Shonpal, Dego, Eric Lau, Kwesi Hagan, Andrew McMillan, Zaahida Nabagereka, James Wilkes, Kayo Chingonyi, Esme Ward, Sarah-Jane Roberts, Valentine Umansky, Deborah Bankole, R.A. Villanueva, Jacob Sam-La Rose, Nikesh Shukla, Vinay Patel, Nishant Kumar, Musa Okwonga and Maria Mendoza.

Finally, to all the mother fuckers, to all the existing power structures that forced this book into being, Fuck y'all.